THE NAVAJOS

A First Americans Book

Virginia Driving Hawk Sneve

illustrated by Ronald Himler

Holiday House/New York

ACKNOWLEDGMENTS

Selections from "Song of the Earth," "Song of the Horse," "Song of the Hogan," "War Song," and "Mountain Songs" are from *The Indians Book* by Natalie Curtis, Dover Publications, Inc., 1968.

The selection from "First Song of Dawn Boy" and the poem of Thomas Littleben is from *Between Sacred Mountains*, Rock Point Community School, Arizona, 1982.

Library of Congress Cataloging-in-Publication Data
Sneve, Virginia Driving Hawk.
The Navajos : a first Americans book / by Virginia Driving Hawk
Sneve ; illustrated by Ronald Himler. — 1st ed.
p.   cm.
Summary: Provides an overview of the history, culture, and ways of
life of the Navaho, or Pueblo, Indians.
ISBN 0-8234-1039-0
1. Navajo Indians — Juvenile literature.   [1. Navajo Indians.
2. Indians of North America — Southwest, New.]   I. Himler, Ronald,
ill.   II. Title.
E99.N3S6   1993   92-40330   CIP   AC
973′.04972 — dc20

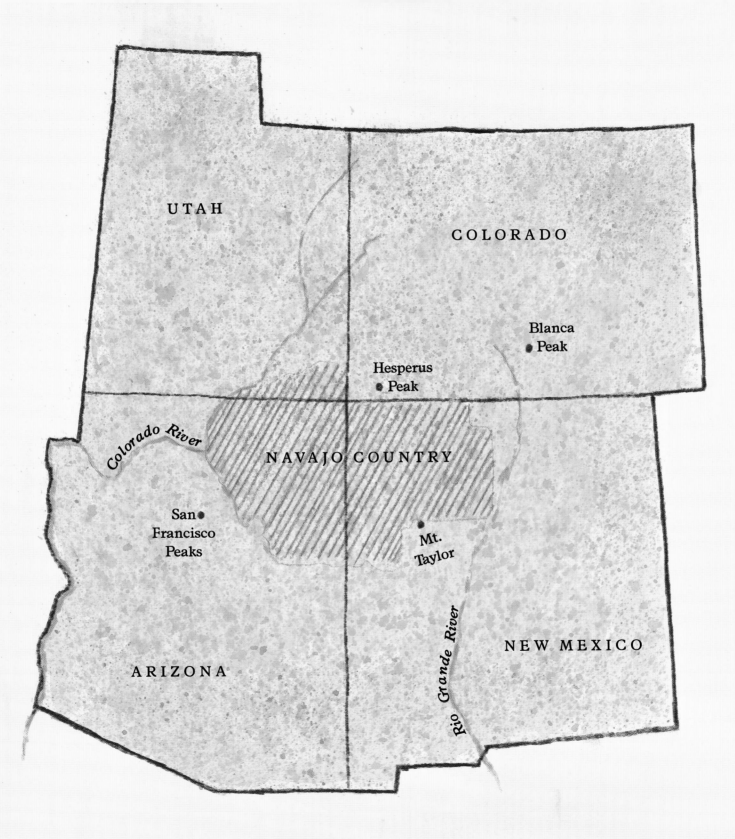

UTAH

COLORADO

Blanca
Peak

Hesperus
Peak

Colorado River

NAVAJO COUNTRY

San
Francisco
Peaks

Mt.
Taylor

Rio Grande River

NEW MEXICO

ARIZONA

CREATION STORY

And the white corn and the yellow corn,
Meeting, joining one another,
Helpmates ever they.
All is beautiful.
from SONG OF THE EARTH

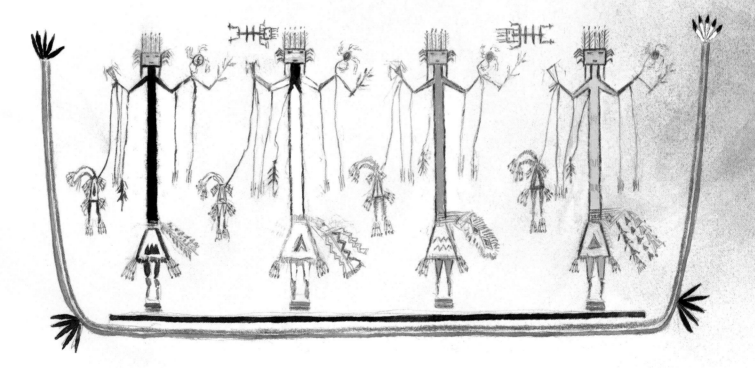

Four tall gods with long bodies appeared out of the earth. They were the Yei, the Holy Ones. The first had a white body; he was Talking God. The second had a blue body; he was Water Bearer. The third had a yellow body; he was House God. The fourth had a black body; he was Fire God.

Water Bearer and Fire God spread a new white buckskin on the ground. Talking God laid an ear of white corn on top of it. House God placed an ear of yellow corn next to it. A white feather was placed under the white ear and a yellow feather under the yellow ear. The Holy Ones covered the corn and feathers with another buckskin.

White Wind came from the east and Yellow Wind from the west. They blew on the skins and lifted them up. The tips of the feathers fluttered in the holy winds. The Yei removed the top buckskin and discovered that the white corn had become a man and the yellow corn had become a woman. The holy winds went into these new bodies and came out of their mouths, so that First Man and First Woman could speak.

First Man and First Woman found a baby girl whom they named Changing Woman. She gave birth to twins who killed the monsters on the earth. Changing Woman traveled to the Pacific Ocean and created four clans of people, from whom the Navajo believe they are descended.

THE HOMELAND

Where my kindred dwell, there I wander.
from FIRST SONG OF DAWN BOY

The Navajos call themselves *Dineh,* "the people." The Dineh traveled eastward from the Pacific coast until they reached what is now Farmington, New Mexico. Much of the territory was occupied by the Ute and Pueblo tribes who later became Navajo enemies. The Dineh broke up into small bands in order to find land to live on.

The Navajo territory of canyons and mesas is known as *Dinetah,* meaning "among the people" or "Navajo homeland."

Scholars believe the Navajos are related to the Athabaskan tribes that live along the northwest Pacific coast and in Canada. Scholars think that the Navajos moved to the Southwest between 1300 and 1600.

THE COMING OF THE
WHITE MEN

Lo, the Turquoise Horse of Johano-ai,
How joyous his neigh.
from SONG OF THE HORSE

rock painting in Canyon de Chelly, Arizona

On canyon walls, Navajos painted pictures of the four holy Yei and of corn, deer, and antelope. They also drew pictures of the first white men they saw. The pictures showed Spanish explorers and missionaries bringing horses, sheep, and cattle from Spain. In the 1600s the Spanish had conquered the Pueblos, the Navajos' neighbors. They turned the Pueblos into slaves, making them care for their horses, sheep, and cattle. The Pueblos also tended the Spaniards' gardens and houses.

The Pueblos did not like this new life, and in 1680 they revolted. The Spaniards who were not killed fled, and their animals escaped to the mountains. The Navajos captured the Spanish horses and sheep and settled in the mountains themselves. They left, however, after their livestock were raided frequently by the Utes, and because of a drought.

By 1750, the Navajos had moved to the valleys and mountains around Canyon de Chelly in northeastern Arizona. Livestock had become part of their life, but the Navajos continued to hunt deer, mountain sheep, antelope, and rabbits. They made their clothing from animal skins. They grew corn, beans, and squash in fields that the Spanish called *Nabaju,* which means "great planted fields." The word *Nabaju* became "Navajo," pronounced "Navaho" in the Spanish way.

In the 1700s, the Navajos used horses for hunting and fighting. Warriors raided Spanish settlers and also other tribes to get more horses, sheep, and goats. Because the Navajos got used to eating mutton, the meat of sheep, they gradually stopped hunting wild animals. They switched to raising livestock and increased their herds. They became wealthy and were feared by other tribes and the white settlers.

FAMILY LIFE

Lo, yonder the hogan,
The hogan blessed.
from SONG OF THE HOGAN

forked-stick hogan

The Navajos did not live in villages as an organized tribe. Instead, individual families lived separately in scattered locations on land that is now New Mexico and Arizona. As the livestock consumed the grass, the families moved to better grazing and farming land. After the grass grew back, a new family sometimes moved into the area left behind. Navajo families did not own the land they farmed and used for grazing. When land was not worked for a season, it was available to others.

Because of their frequent moves, a Navajo home was easy and quick to build and was called a "forked-stick hogan." It was built of three supporting poles and covered with mud and brush. The door always faced the east to welcome the early morning light.

Later, the Navajos built more permanent hogans, made of logs and chinked with mud. They were designed in the shape of a circle or octagon.

The Navajos believed that bad spirits were present in a hogan after a person died. So, to avoid the bad spirits, they would leave the hogan and build a new one. To make sure there were no bad spirits there, they held a ceremony to bless the new home.

permanent hogan

Each family set up a loom in the hogan or, in the summer, outside under a brush shelter. The women learned to spin wool and cotton into yarn and to dye fabric using natural colors. Now the Navajos' clothing, except for moccasins, was no longer made of animal skins. The women's dresses were made of two blankets sewn at the shoulders and belted at the waist. The men wore cotton shirts and trousers. The children's clothes looked like the adults'. The Navajos had everything they needed from their land and livestock or from trading.

Because individual families lived so far apart, the Navajos had no single tribal leader. The family groups each had a local headman, but he had no power over families in other locations. The men were the protectors and would band together to defend their families.

A Navajo grandmother was the center of family life. The children belonged to her and to her clan. The women had power because they owned the sheep. When a child was four to six years old, he or she was given a lamb. Now the boy or girl was no longer considered a child and began to learn adult responsibilities.

Both boys and girls were expected to care for the sheep. They would let the sheep out of the corral in the early morning and herd the flock to a grassy area. In the evening they brought the sheep home.

When a girl married, her mother gave her some sheep of her own. Her new husband also had sheep from his mother to take to his new home. The bride's relatives built the young couple a hogan near her mother's house.

CEREMONY

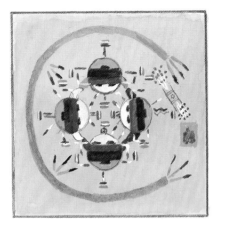

All is beautiful,
All is beautiful,
All is beautiful, indeed.
from SONG OF THE EARTH

a sand painting of "Four Houses of the Sun"

The Navajos believe that everything in the universe has a purpose and a special place. There is good within all things, but evil and danger can result when the normal balance of the universe is disturbed. For example, when a person gets sick, it is not because of germs, but because evil has been released. To restore order, a medicine man or singer is asked to hold a "sing" or ceremony performed according to exact rules. He learns the ritual words and sand paintings by studying with older medicine men for many years.

There are ceremonies that may last several nights to protect families, homes, sheep, and crops, and to heal. The Navajos believe the Yei, the Holy Ones, are attracted by the ritual songs, prayers, stories, and paintings. If the Holy Ones are pleased with the way the ceremony has gone, they will "set things right" and restore the balance.

The singer may create several sand paintings or sacred pictures during the ceremony. He uses crushed sandstone, corn pollen, or the charcoal of a tree that has been struck by lightning. He trickles these fine grains from his hand into a special design that depicts the Holy Ones. He rubs out one painting and carries away the sand before starting a new one.

IN BATTLE

One upon another, dashed to earth;
Lo, the flint youth, he am I.

from WAR SONG

The Navajos' land belonged to Mexico until 1848, when a treaty made it part of the United States. Then American white men came to look for silver and gold, and fighting broke out. The Navajos had been fighting the Utes and Pueblos, but now they had to battle the white men also. In 1848 U.S. soldiers came to Santa Fe, New Mexico, to get the Indians to sign a treaty to stop the fighting. A few Navajo headmen signed the treaty, but they were not chiefs who had authority over the whole tribe. Most of the Navajos did not recognize the treaty as having any power over them.

To enforce the treaty, the U.S. Army in 1851 built Fort Defiance in the center of Navajo territory. From the fort, U.S. soldiers tried to subdue the Navajos, but the Indians fought back. In 1863 Colonel Kit Carson followed orders to kill the Navajo warriors and to capture the women and children. His troops also burned fields and hogans and killed thousands of sheep. When winter came, the Navajos had no homes or food, and 8,000 surrendered at Fort Defiance.

From Fort Defiance the Navajos were forced to march 300 miles to Fort
Sumner, New Mexico. This was called "The Long Walk." During that cold
journey, more than 300 Navajos died from exhaustion or disease. Others were
shot by the soldiers.

At Fort Sumner, the Navajos were crowded into land that was reserved for them and from which they could not leave. They were expected to farm on this reservation, but the soil was poor, and many Indians died of hunger. The Comanche who lived in the area raided and killed the Navajos, and a smallpox epidemic killed 2,000 more in a few months.

RESETTLEMENT

squash blossom necklace

In life unending, and beyond it
Yea, seated at home behold me.
from MOUNTAIN SONGS

In June 1868, the Navajos were permitted to leave Fort Sumner and return to their former homeland, which was now a reservation. This reservation is in parts of present-day Arizona, Utah, and New Mexico. The Navajos are the largest of all North American tribes.

The Navajos resettled in their lands and were very poor. They could farm, but gardens did not grow well in the dry land. The U.S. government gave them flocks of sheep, but because the Navajos could not herd them to new pastures when the grass was eaten, they could only have small flocks. Their farms and flocks couldn't support them, and the government had to give them food and clothing.

From Mexicans, the men learned to be silversmiths. They made buttons and jewelry from nickels, dimes, and quarters because they did not understand that money could buy things. They also used turquoise in the jewelry. White traders set up stores on the reservation, and the Navajos learned that they could trade their jewelry for cloth and other items they did not have.

The women liked the velveteen material they got from the traders. They learned to sew the fabric into blouses that they trimmed with silver jewelry. Both men and women wore silver concha belts decorated with silver disks. When the Navajo found out that money was needed to buy food and other items, they began selling their silver and turquoise jewelry.

The women learned that they could make money by trading their homespun weaving to traders who sold it throughout the nation. The Navajo became famous for their beautiful rugs, blankets, and jewelry.

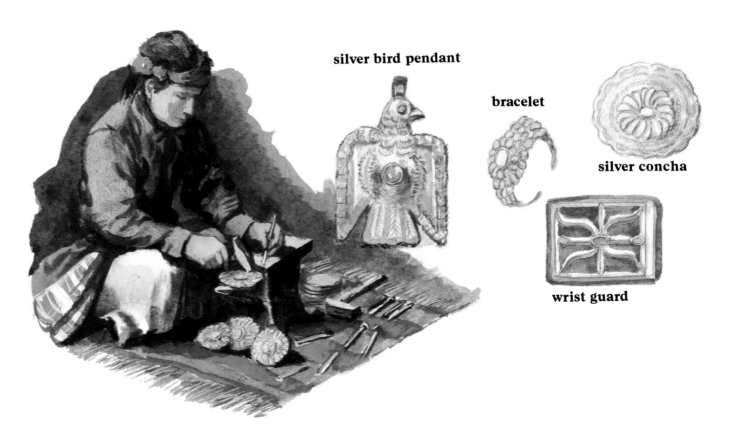

silver bird pendant

bracelet

silver concha

wrist guard

THE NAVAJOS TODAY

Now of Unending life,
Thereof he telleth.
from MOUNTAIN SONGS

Today some Navajos weave blankets and rugs and make jewelry. These beautiful goods are sold all over the world.

Although a few modern Navajos prefer to live in hogans, most have frame or brick houses and dwell in villages. Some families don't have horses and sheep anymore, but in those that do, the mother still owns the animals.

The children go to schools that are controlled by the local community. Navajo history and language are taught so that the children will know and value their tribal traditions. There is a tribal college for young people and adults to attend, but many high-school graduates attend colleges and universities away from the reservation. There are Navajo doctors, nurses, lawyers, and teachers on the reservation. Other Navajos live and work in cities all over the United States.

The Navajos now elect a president to lead a central tribal government which makes decisions for the whole tribe, but the people continue to belong to clans. Many of the men work for the gas and coal companies that have been set up on the reservation. The tribe needs the income from these companies, but the Navajos are concerned about the way mining and energy production are hurting the land.

I am sitting outside my hogan.
I am thinking,
Looking at the red rocks,
the ridges, the sheep,
the plants,
and all in my world.
I am thinking
What it will be like here
In the Future.

THOMAS LITTLEBEN,
ROCK POINT SCHOOL

The Navajos believe that all people must live in harmony with the earth. If the earth is taken care of, it will always be there to provide for the people.

I see the earth
I am looking at Her and smile
Because She makes me happy.
The Earth, looking back at me
Is smiling too.
May I walk happily
And lightly
On Her.

from SONG OF THE EARTH

AUTHOR'S NOTE

The Navajo creation story is long with many variations. The one I've used here is only a small part of the whole story.

There are several hundreds of Navajo songs that have special purposes. Because the songs were translated from Navajo into English by different scholars, they too have many variations. In the lines I've used from "Song of the Horse," *Johano-ai* is the sun.

The information in this book barely touches on Navajo history, culture, and present life. For more in-depth information, contact the Navajo Curriculum Center, Rough Rock Demonstration School, Rough Rock, AZ 86503.

INDEX